VEGAN ABCS WITH BREAD BUNSON
Coloring Book

For best results, use crayons or colored pencils

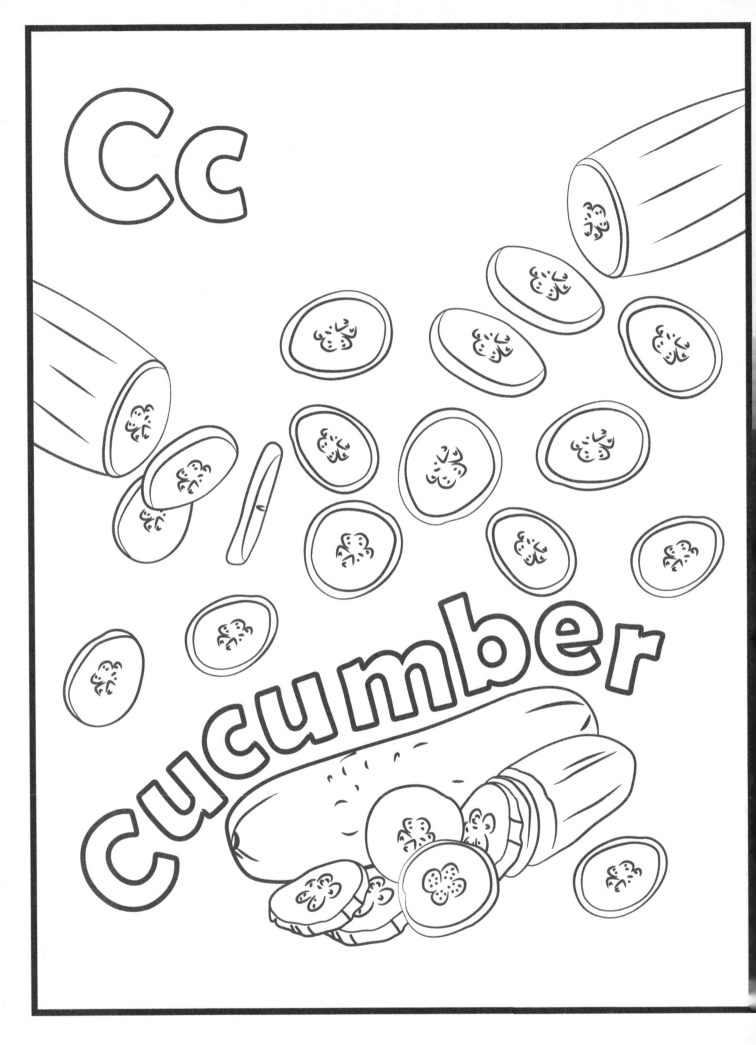

Ee

Elderberry

Syrup

Time to get better!

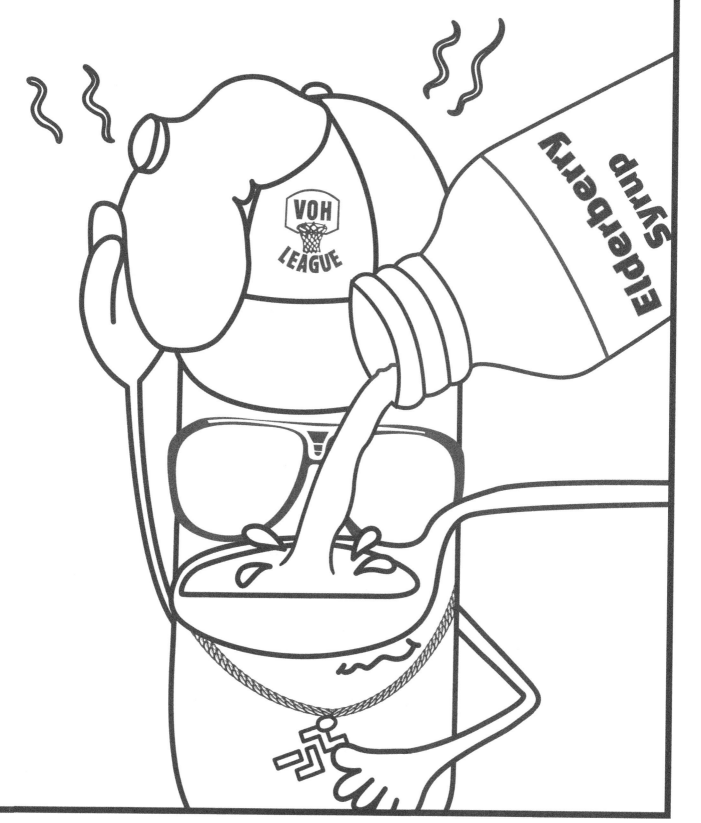

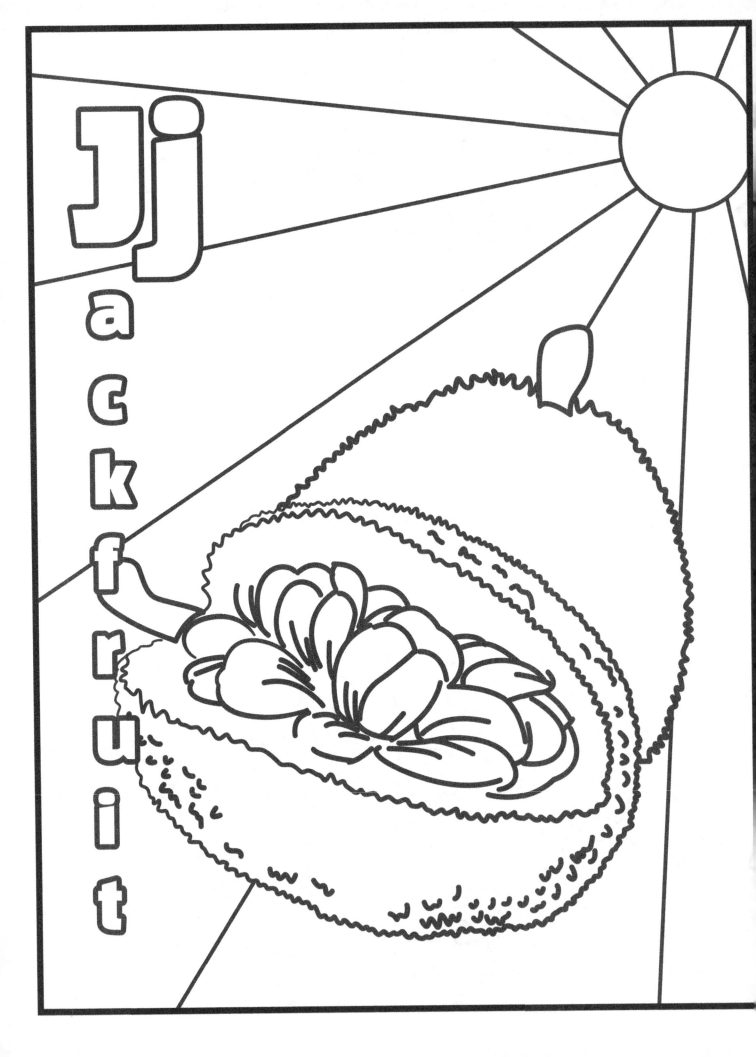

Kk

kale

Plant
Power

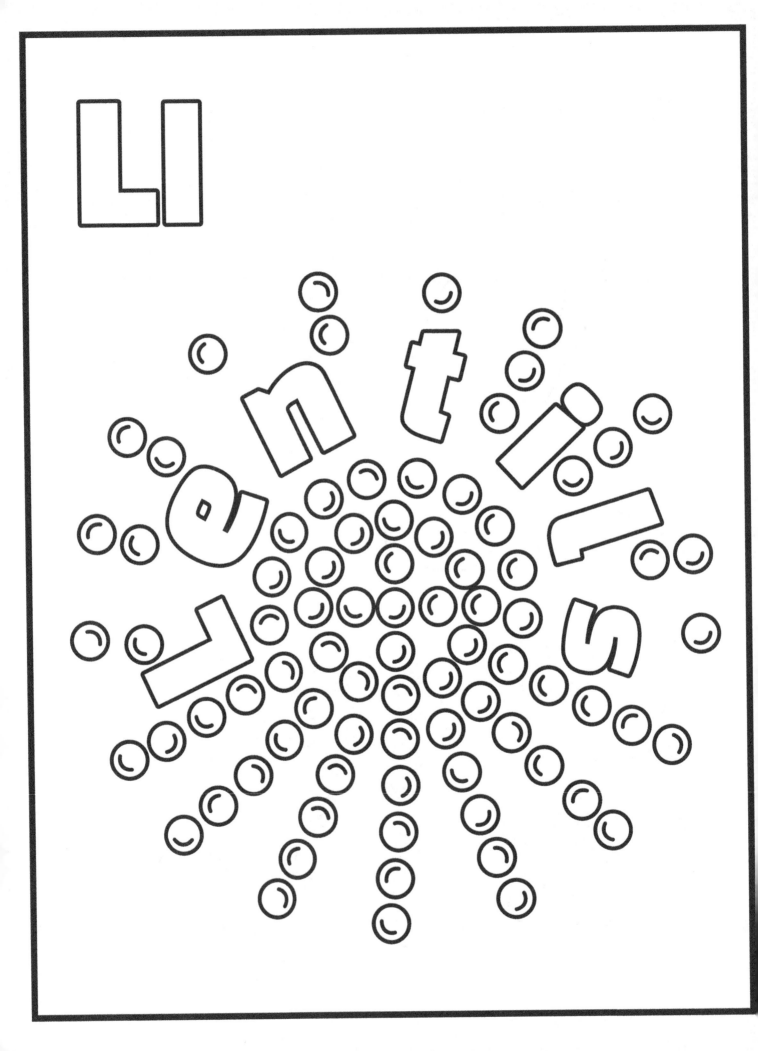

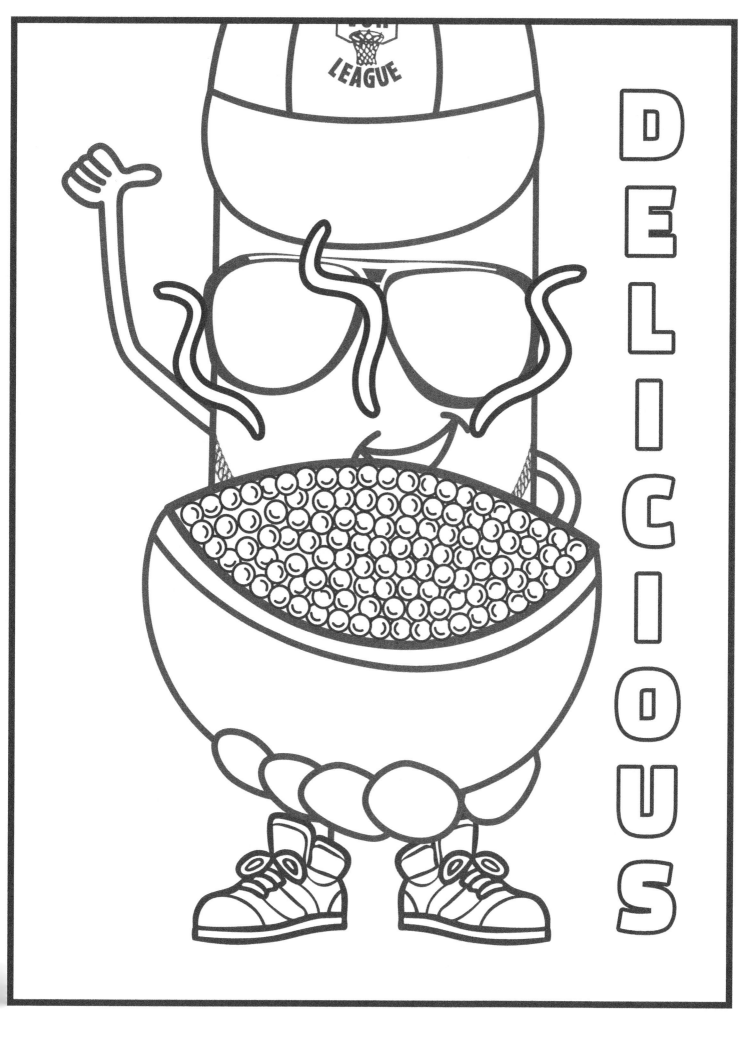

Turkey
← Tail

Lion's
← Mane

Portobello

ORGANIC QUINOA

PURPLE
VEGAN
MOMMa

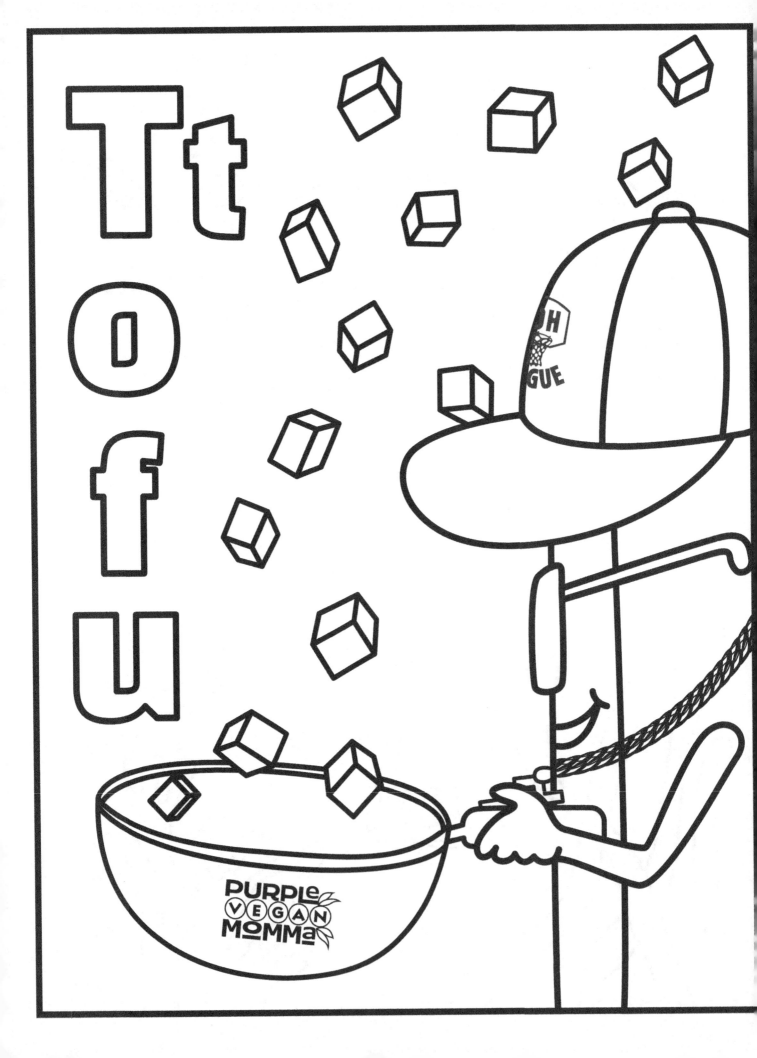

Vv

VEGGIE

Ww

Walnuts

1. Crack

2. Open

3. Enjoy

Lesson By : Bread Bunson

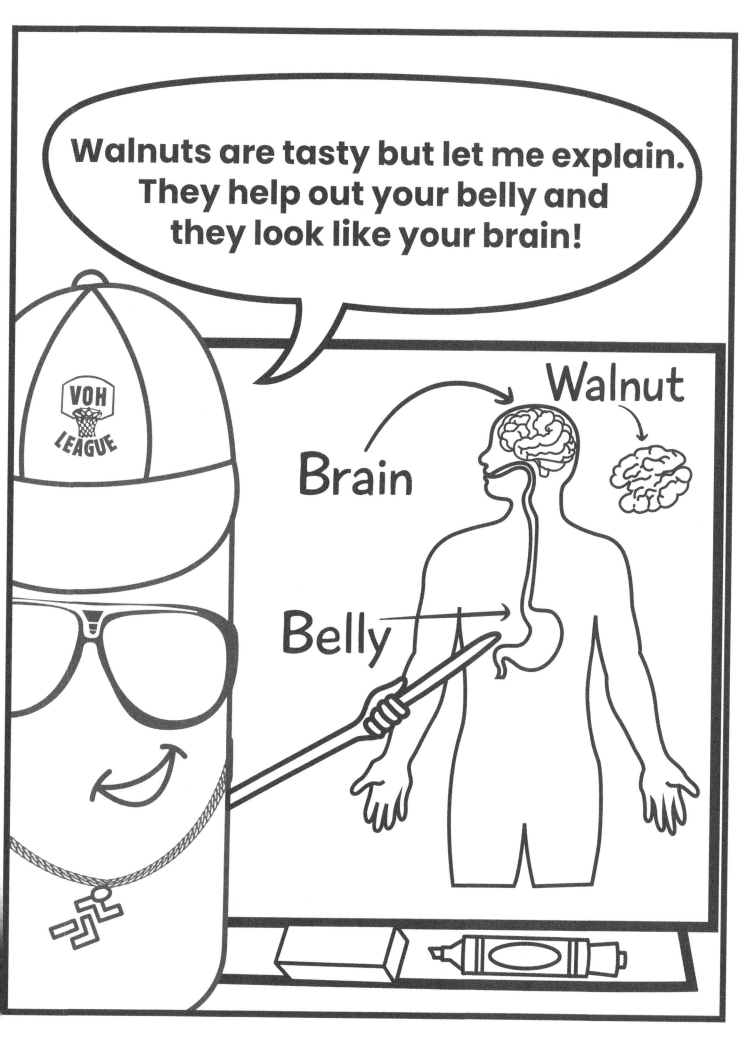

It's a natural sweetener made from Birch wood...
Add it to your syrup or gum it's all good!
-Bread Bunson

Behind the Logos

Founded in 2020, Purple Vegan Momma
aims to promote a healthy lifestyle for all ages through books, toys,
and educational cartoons. The combination of dietary, emotional,
and expressive intelligence gives us the key to a happy
and healthy life. When we eat better we think better!
@purpleveganmomma
www.purpleveganmomma.com

VOH was founded in 2013 in Haverstraw,
NY by Bread Bronson.
Since then it has grown into the #1 basketball league
in the Hudson Valley 845 NY area.
#VOHBasketball #NeverTuckYourTown
www.vohleague.com

Founded in 2019, MOR Apparel is a unique athletic
apparel company providing clients with the proper gear
to #DoMOR for themselves and their communities.
@mor_apparel_us
www.morapparelus.com

Family owned and operated since 2018.
The Collier Luxury Company seamlessly weaves together art,
intelligence, and functionality for its own brand of luxury.
Material goods are nice but family is the greatest luxury in life.
#familyisluxury
@thecollierluxurycompany
www.collierluxurycompany.com

Made in the USA
Middletown, DE
01 December 2023

43156274R00031